Stylish
SUCCULENTS

Japanese Inspired Container Gardens for Small Spaces

TOKIIRO

TUTTLE Publishing

Tokyo | Rutland, Vermont | Singapore

Contents

04 Succulents are Dynamic

06 CHAPTER 1
A Little Universe in a Pot:
Planting Succulents in Containers

08 Basic Tools and Materials
10 Basic Methods for Planting
13 A Little Composition That Fits in the Palm of Your Hand
14 Reaching to the Sky
16 Planting in a Container with No Holes
22 A City Veiled in Red
23 Life Passed Down
24 Immeasurable Vitality
26 A New Star is Born
27 A Landscape Where a Guardian Deity Resides

28 On Wild Earth
29 A Mystical Forest
34 The Power of Vitality and Evolution
35 Celebrating Shadows
36 The Gentleness of Pink; A Jewel on a Moonlit Night
37 Mr Rabbit, What Did You See That Made You Jump?
38 The Flowers of Succulent Plants
40 Memory
41 Quietly Listening to the Voices of Plants

42 CHAPTER 2
Using Succulents to Add Color to Walls:
Creating Wreaths and Tableaux

48 How to Make a Succulent Wreath
   Using Succulents to Add Color to Walls
57 Seasonal Color
58 Tranquil Eternity
60 The World's Most Enduring Greenery
61 Just Like a Corsage
62 Wreath Made with Air Plants
64 How to Make a Tableau Wall Hanging
69 A Pop-out Picture

70 **CHAPTER 3**
Floating in the Air:
Hanging Succulents

74 A Forgotten Forest
76 Prepare the Container for Hanging
79 Three Spacecraft Flying Through the Air
80 Leaving Home

A Guide to Succulents
18 ❶ Succulents That Grow Vertically
20 ❷ Succulents That Spread Out
30 ❸ Rosette Types
32 ❹ Enjoying Haworthia
44 ❺ Succulents for Wreaths
72 ❻ Succulents That are Ideal for Hanging

81 **CHAPTER 4**
Living with Succulents

82 What is a Succulent?
83 Succulents Love Water!
Photosynthesis Prompts a Love of Water
84 Creating an Environment to Promote Photosynthesis
85 Photosynthesis in Succulents Differs from That in Other Plants
86 Succulents are Not Good Indoor Dwellers
Light, Air and Water are Vital for Succulents
87 The Charm of Succulents
The Beauty of Succulents' Fall Colors
88 The Growth Pattern of Succulents
A Little More About the Importance of Sunlight
89 Cultivating and Planting Tips for Succulents by Genus

90 *Q&A: How to Grow Succulents Successfully*
92 *Our Own Journey with Succulents*
93 *To Our Readers*

Succulents are Dynamic

Always remember that. The succulent you see now is ever-changing—a fleeting image that reflects its current environment. These plants respond to their surroundings—tomorrow; the day after; a week, month or year from now, they'll sport a fresh new look. They are never really complete. They are constantly evolving.

At Tokiiro, we contemplate succulents from every angle so that our arrangements will celebrate the plants' transformation over time. They resemble ikebana in the way they conjure up a world unfolding in space, and bonsai in the snapshot of scenery they offer.

For Tokiiro, a plant container is like a sheet of drawing paper or a canvas. Succulents are the pastels, colored pencils and paints. We plant them as if drawing a picture inspired by a memory in the mind's eye, or by the container's small inner space (or outer space). Without the space created by the container, expression is impossible. The variations in the glazes and forms of the pots enhance the individuality of the "universes" created.

The pencils, paints and pastels that color these container universes aren't anything special; they're simply the materials at hand. In other words, the succulents used aren't hard-to-find hybrids; rather, they're what could be called garden varieties.

The motifs we draw are narrow lanes traversed in country adventures; mountain ranges that rise up above fields; the claw of a crayfish; deep forests in which ponds turn up out of nowhere. Somehow, matched with containers and succulents, these memories and imaginings have become little gardens and forests that evoke warm feelings of nostalgia.

What kind of picture will you paint with succulents?

A Little Universe in a Pot
Planting Succulents in Containers

Outer space is free of boundaries. Tokiiro thinks of plant arrangements in the same way. Because succulents have an incredibly strong life force, by responding to their environments they evolve over time to achieve their unique forms. Each succulent you plant in a little pot evokes a new world that far exceeds human imagination. That new world, too, continues to evolve. In it is a beauty that only time can create. In tiny pots, arrangements of succulents give birth to a world view thousands of times bigger than themselves. Try imagining this view of nature when planting succulents in containers.

Basic Tools and Materials

Let's begin by talking about the tools you'll need to create arrangements of succulents. There's nothing that's particularly hard to obtain—it's easy to make a start as these are all items that can be found at home or in a home center.

1 Mesh
Placed over the hole in the base, mesh prevents soil from trickling out of the bottom of the container. Use mesh sold at home centers for security doors, cutting it with scissors to the size of the container base.

5 Spatula
Use to pack soil in firmly in the container. A small version, such as a wooden coffee stir stick, is easy to use as its narrow shape and smoothness are just right.

2 Container
The flower pot used for arrangements. In order to ensure good drainage, a pot with a hole in the base is recommended. However, as long as watering is carried out correctly, a container without a hole is fine too. There are also ways to make holes in containers (see p10).

6 Wire
Bend wire into a U-shape to secure succulents into soil if they're tall or otherwise unstable. Use 24-gauge florist wire (preferably brown, to blend in with the soil). Florist wire is fairly rust-resistant.

3 Scissors
Use for cutting mesh to size, trimming succulents and so on. Easy-to-use craft scissors are fine.

7 Scoop
Use to pour dirt into a container. If creating an arrangement in a coffee cup or small container, a small scoop is handy.

4 Tweezers
Useful when planting small succulent sproutings in between gaps. Rather than gardening tweezers, use the type with bent tips intended for detailed work.

8 Soil
Use soil for succulents which is sold at home centers, gardening stores and so on. Plants in the Crassulaceae family in particular have delicate roots, so use fine soil.

Basic Methods for Planting

1. Prepare the Container

Find a container you'd like to use. If the base has a hole, place mesh over it (for containers without holes, see below and p16). A small container is pleasing to look at and makes for an easy first arrangement. Try using a coffee cup or other small container that appeals to you to make the finished arrangement all the more charming.

Cut mesh to the size of the container base and place in container.

Fill container with soil to about ⅓ of its height.

HOW TO MAKE A HOLE IN A CONTAINER

A container that doesn't have a hole in its base is fine to use as it is, but a hole allows water to drain well, making it easier to create a compatible environment for these plants. You'll need an electric drill. Start with a fine drill bit, monitoring the hole and gradually increasing to thicker bits as you go. If you're using a large container, it's better to make several smaller holes rather than one large one.

1. Start by using an extremely fine bit and drilling from the outside of the container. 2. Change to a thicker drill bit as you go, if necessary. 3. Once the drill seems as if it will break through the surface, turn the container over and drill from the inside. 4. Drill from the outside again to adjust and increase the size of the hole. 5. Depending on the size of the container, make several holes ⅜ inch (1 cm) in diameter. However, if the base of the container is thin, it may crack, so take care and don't drill too many holes.

2. Prepare the Succulents

Divide the succulents to be used in the arrangement and place them on a tray. There are three methods of division, as shown below, with each method appropriate for different plant types. If you're using the bouquet method suggested by Tokiiro (see p12), leave soil attached to roots.

Sedum Oaxacanum
This type of Sedum grows comparatively tall and sends out buds at the sides. The edges of its leaves are dusted with a white powder.

Acre Aureum
A member of the Sedum genus, the new buds at the tips of its leaves turn lemon yellow as winter approaches, brightening up arrangements that feature it. It soon weakens if it dries out, so make sure not to cut its roots when planting.

Harmsii
Genus Echeveria. In winter, the leaves are attractive, turning wine red to resemble velvet. Plants that have been growing for some time have straight trunks, creating an impressive feature in an arrangement.

Momiji Matsuri
(Red leaf festival) Genus Crassulaceae. As the name suggests, these plants turn red in winter, creating accents in arrangements of succulents. They grow rapidly from spring to fall, forming many new buds at the base of the leaves. If trimmed off, these can be used as cuttings to easily increase stock.

Sedum Pachyphyllum
Genus Sedum. Known as "Maiden's mind" in Japan, its name likely comes from the blush of red at the tips of its leaves. It spreads from buds along its sides and can be made to resemble a bonsai.

METHODS OF DIVISION

For succulents with new stock plants that are small and have delicate stems, use tweezers with bent ends to carefully pull plants out of the soil.

For plants that have grown to fill the pot, draw the succulent out of the pot and hold it at the roots with both hands. Brush off soil to see where the plants are joined, then divide them carefully so as not to damage the roots.

In the case that the stock plant has not grown very large, grip at the roots using tweezers and pull it up carefully so as not to damage the

roots. If unable to raise it out of the soil, use the methods of division at left.

3. Create a Form as If Putting Together a Bouquet

This method involves arranging succulents in your hand as if putting together a bouquet, then planting in a container.
Create the look of a world where time has elapsed by winding the succulents around one another as they would grow naturally after a while.

Consider the overall balance of the arrangement as you put succulents together.

Once the arrangement is ready, place it in the container and make necessary changes to aspects such as the volume of foliage and the overall flow. Use scissors to trim arrangement to desired shape for planting.

4. Add the Soil

Once you've decided on the form of the arrangement, hold the plants gently in one hand in the container and add soil in from the side. Make sure not to lift the plants up out of the pot but rather keep them securely in place as you do this. As the soil needs to be packed in firmly, this is the task that takes the most time.

Hold plants in place while gently adding soil in at the side. Press soil in by working the spatula up and down. Keep adding soil and pressing it in with the spatula to stabilize plants.

You'll need quite a lot of soil. Once soil has been added, consider the overall composition, turning the pot around to view it from all aspects. Use tweezers to add extra plants in any gaps, making adjustments until you're satisfied.

A Little Composition That Fits in the Palm of Your Hand

Tokiiro's succulent arrangements are small and companionable. We also like to decide on a theme and build around it, just like visualizing what you want to draw and how you'll draw it before actually putting paint to canvas. Having a theme in mind makes arranging succulents more fun. The arrangements on the following pages serve as examples, so please refer to them for ideas on how to build on your vision. Watering techniques will be discussed on page 25.

Container Garden 1

Reaching to the Sky

Up in the sky… what kind of world is up there?
For sure, it's a world where unimaginable beauty abounds…
The sky-blue color of the cup entices you to look up at the
world above, so the succulents selected here are mainly the
sort that grow straight up towards the sky.

PLANTS USED
Sedum pachyphyllum (Genus Sedum)
Echeveria carnicolor (with flower buds; Genus Echeveria)
Crassula lycopodioides (Genus Crassulaceae)
Kalanchoe eriophylla (Genus Kalanchoe)
Momiji matsuri (Genus Crassulaceae)
Sedum oaxacanum (Genus Sedum)
Graptopetalum bronze (Genus Graptopetalum)
Echeveria white rose (Genus Echeveria)

GROWING TIP
We've used an attractive coffee mug and miniature pitcher in this
arrangement, neither of which have holes in their base. When using
containers without holes, it's important to control the amount of water
given. Please refer to p25 for information on watering.

Planting in a Container with No Holes

1. Prepare the Container

Spread stones over the entire base of the container. Doing this creates gaps which improves air flow around the roots, helps to prevent root decay, and aids root development. Take the size of the pot into account, but aim to add roughly 2 inches (5 cm) of soil to cover the stones at the bottom.

2. Prepare the Succulents

Prepare the succulents you've selected. It's a good idea to prepare more than are required as this allows for more freedom of expression.

1. Sedum pachyphyllum (Genus Sedum) 2. Graptopetalum bronze (Genus Graptopetalum) 3. Crassula lycopodioides (Genus Crassulaceae) 4. Acre aureum (Genus Sedum) 5. Snow (Genus Sedeveria) 6. Momiji matsuri (Genus Crassulaceae) 7. Lola (Genus Echeveria) 8. Debbie (Genus Graptoveria) 9. Sedum oaxacanum 10. Echeveria carnicolor (Genus Echeveria) 11. Harmsii (Genus Echeveria) 12. Kalanchoe eriophylla (Genus Kalanchoe)

3. First Position the Main Plants

Depending on the theme, start by planting the main plants. In this example, the theme is "reaching to the sky" so plants that grow vertically form the centerpiece. Plants that grow vertically such as Sedum pachyphyllum have bulk to them and are difficult to balance, so in order to increase their stability, you have to secure them with soil.

Decide where to position the main plants and secure them with soil.

Bend wire into a U shape to create a U pin.

Wedge the stem into the U pin and poke the pin into the soil. Use a pin on either side of the plant to secure it.

4. Place the Other Plants Around the Main Plants as If Creating a Bouquet

Gather the remaining succulents in the palm of your hand like a bouquet and plant them in the container, scooping the soil and packing it in as shown on p12. Consider the overall balance as you work the other plants in around the main ones.

Succulents That Grow Vertically

Crassula Lycopodioides
Genus Crassulaceae. Grows vertically, sending out buds all the way up the stem. It remains green all year round, so it's easy to work its form and color into arrangements.

Kalanchoe Eriophylla
Genus Kalanchoe. The hairs on the leaves are white and remain relatively the same color all year round, making it a suitable plant to use when white is desired. It is relatively strong and easy to cultivate type.

Echeveria Carnicolor
Genus Echeveria. Echeveria have long flower buds with blooms at the end. Make use of their height in arrangements. The flowers bloom for a long time.

Vertically-growing succulents can be used in arrangements to resemble huge trees standing solo on a vast plain, or a jungle in which one has lost one's way, and so on. They also can be used as accents in an arrangement to express the movement of clouds and lightning, waves, animals, dragons and more. Echeveria stock plants that have been left for a while and plants in the Crassulaceae genus grow relatively quickly. In the Sedum genus too there are plants that move in interesting ways, such as the Sedum pachyphyllum with foliage that grows at the end of a stem.

Harmsii
Genus Echeveria. The stems resemble tree trunks. With some time, a sense of movement forms. They make good seedlings.

Tetragona
Genus Crassulaceae. These plants shed their lower leaves as they grow upwards. They grow relatively tall, so keep this in mind when planting.

Sedum Pachyphyllum
Genus Sedum. There's no doubt that these plants, with their foliage at the end of stems resembling bonsai, are the stars in any arrangement. Make sure to play up their free-flowing form.

Succulents That Spread Out

Eurema Mexicana
(Genus Sedum)

Sedum Makinoi
(Genus Sedum)

Acre Aureum
(Genus Sedum)

Little Missy
(Genus Crassulaceae)

Sedum Japonicum 'Morimura'
(Genus Sedum)

Purple Haze
(Genus Crassulaceae)

Even within the Sedum genus, some types such as the stonecrops have small leaves that grow not at the ends of stems but along the sides, creating ground cover as they increase. A similarly spreading type can be found in the Crassulaceae genus, which allows for combining the plants within an arrangement. The various colors make gradation possible.

Sedum Oryzifolium
(Genus Sedum)

Makinoi Ogon
(Genus Sedum)

Pallidum
(Genus Sedum)

**Sedum Mexicanum
Green Mound**
(Genus Sedum)

Ground Cover Plants
(Genus Sedum)

Sedum Uniflorum
(Genus Sedum)

PLANTS USED
Momiji matsuri (Genus Crassulaceae)
Sedum rubrotinctum (Genus Sedum)
Acre aureum (Genus Sedum)

PLANTING TIP
These succulents are red as they change color in the fall. Imagine a cool breeze blowing by, quietly embraced by the scenery, and maintain a feeling of calm as you face the container to create this vision.

GROWING TIP
Succulents sense the season through the changes in temperature between day and night, among other means. Make sure to let them stay connected to nature by allowing them to feel the outside air.

Container Garden 2

A City Veiled in Red

Colors change with the seasons in this city. Now, it's veiled in red as the midwinter sun casts shadows, embracing winter rather than longing for the coming of spring: this is the image we have tried to create here. In summer, it will be transformed into a city cloaked in green.

Container Garden 3

Life Passed Down

The life force in a succulent plant is truly amazing. A leaf that falls from a stem can put out roots. A new bud forms from something that seemed dead. Succulents teach us a lot about the wonder of life.

PLANTS USED
Party dress (Genus Echeveria)
Crassula mesembrianthoides (Genus Crassulaceae)
Sedum pachyphyllum (Genus Sedum)
Sedum rubrotinctum (Genus Sedum)
Sedum spathulifolium ssp. pruinosum (Genus Sedum)
Sedum japonicum 'morimura' (Genus Sedum)
Senecio rowleyanus (Family Zsteraceae, Genus Senecio)

PLANTING TIP
Start by planting the Party dress first as it is the centerpiece. Keep in mind how the plants' growth over time will affect the arrangement and plant vertically growing succulents beside trailing succulents to create balance as plant coverage increases.

GROWING TIP
Plants in the Sedum genus with small leaves love water. They dry out easily, so check the soil and leaves daily and water accordingly. Constant attention is the key to growing them well.

Immeasurable Vitality

When it comes to succulents, a life force dwells even in a single easily-plucked leaf. Place one on top of dry soil and after two to three months it should grow roots and buds. That's just one of the appealing aspects of succulents.

ABOVE Roots and buds growing from a fallen leaf. Once the roots have started emerging, plant the leaf in soil to cultivate the plant.

BELOW When the plant puts out new buds, the old leaves on the lower part of the stem may wither and die. This does not mean anything is wrong with the plant, so don't be alarmed. This phenomenon occurs because in order to develop, the new buds need moisture which the old leaves supply. In this way, one generation of leaves makes way for the next.

Sprouting New Buds
from Fallen Leaves

In the course of creating arrangements, leaves often fall off, but don't worry—placed like this on top of soil, they'll generate a new life.

Place on top of dry soil. Fleshy leaves such as those of the Echeveria genus only need to be placed on top of dry soil—there's no need to embed them in the soil or water them. They'll put out roots in two to three months.

Leaves damaged through stress. Plants can experience various kinds of stress from extremes in heat or cold, lack of oxygen, excessive humidity and so on. Be aware of changes in surroundings where the leaves are placed.

Plant leaf cuttings in soil The leaves of succulents such as Sedum pachyphyllum (left) and Crassula lycopodioides (right) can be planted in soil to increase stock plants. Plants increase differently depending on their genus, so try to remember how each genus generates new stock.

How to Water Arrangements
of Succulents

There's no need to water when creating an arrangement! Succulents are susceptible to stress, so in order to settle them into the surroundings in their new container, hold off on watering for a week and place them in a sunny spot outdoors. A week after planting, give them plenty of water, and a week after that, feel the soil and look at its condition. If it's moist, it means it's not suited to the current location, so move the container to somewhere conducive to photosynthesis such as a spot that receives a lot of sun. Once the soil is dry, wait another week before watering. It doesn't matter if water gets on the leaves, but some if water collects around the base of their leaves some plants can rot or it may make it difficult for the leaves to breathe, so it's best to aim water at the soil. Splash plenty of water over containers with holes in the base, but be careful not to overwater for container that have no holes. Give them about a third of the container's volume in water.

Watering schedule

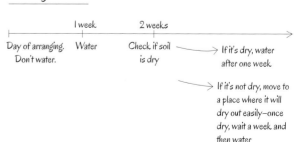

A New Star is Born

A cloud of gas surrounding a clear blue earth
creates the fluctuating world of a newborn planet.
It appears that this new planet hosts new life—
floating into view comes the glowing white
Kalanchoe eriophylla with its white life.

PLANTS USED
Kalanchoe eriophylla (Genus Kalanchoe)
Momiji matsuri (Genus Crassulaceae)
Crassula capitella (Genus Crassulaceae)

PLANTING TIP
White plants are something of a rarity. The
glistening of the white hairs on their leaves
as the sun touches them creates an aura of
holiness. New life is born, and clad in their
fall colors, Momiji matsuri and Crassula
capitella support its increasing vitality.

GROWING TIP
This is a relatively easy combination to grow.
However, if the correct balance of sunlight
and water isn't maintained, the whiteness
of Kalanchoe eriophylla can be affected, so
make sure to keep an eye on its condition.

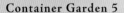
Container Garden 5

A Landscape Where a Guardian Deity Resides

The red Kalanchoe thyrsiflora has managed to get this big after growing as a new shoot from a cutting. Watching over things from above like a protector, its huge leaves envelop the scenery.

PLANTS USED
Kalanchoe thyrsiflora (Genus Kalanchoe)
Sedum makinoii (Genus Sedum)
Crassula lycopodioides (Genus Crassulaceae)

PLANTING TIP
A single Kalanchoe thyrsiflora is placed in the center of the container. To emphasize the fact that the small leaves at the bottom of the plant will inherit its life, evergreen succulents have been planted around it.

GROWING TIP
Makinoi does not cope well with heat or humidity, so take care during hot summer days. Place it in a well ventilated spot or create a breeze near it by using an electric fan.

On Wild Earth

Even in the harshest places, plants continue to survive. These plants put out "aerial roots" from their branches that become genuine roots when they reach the ground. They're a brilliant example of how plants can seek and acquire the means to survive on the tiniest amount of nutrients.

PLANTS USED
Aeonium haworthii Tricolor (Genus Aeonium)
Sedum uniflorum (Genus Sedum)

PLANTING TIP
The Aeonium haworthii Tricolor is planted in such a way as to play up its aerial roots, with succulents that spread over the ground accompanying it in this arrangement. The aerial roots appear to connect heaven and earth. At a glance, it looks like a bonsai, don't you think?

GROWING TIP
As Aenium haworthii Tricolor does not cope well with high temperatures and humidity, make sure to place it somewhere well ventilated in summer. With plenty of sunlight and time, it's possible to grow a compact plant similar to a bonsai.

Container Garden 7
A Mystical Forest

Deep, deep in the mountains where no one has ventured before lies a dimly lit forest in which some plants make their way up, up to the tiny bit of light that reaches them, while others trail down, down, the combination creating a veritable paradise for plants. This is where nature's true form can be found.

PLANTS USED
Crassula lycopodioides (Genus Crassulaceae)
Green pet (Genus Sedum)
Senecio prymidatuabar (Family Asteraceae, Genus Senecio)
Acre aureum (Genus Sedum)

PLANTING TIP
In order to evoke a forest, succulents are planted to fill the container and twist around each other. The vertically growing Crassula lycopodioides is straight and tall while the trailing Acre aureum is allowed to hang down naturally. Make an effort to play up the plants' inherent "flow."

GROWING TIP
In the same Asteraceae family as Senecio rowleyanus, Senecio prymidatuabar requires plenty of water and becomes weak if it doesn't receive enough. Consider the other succulents in the arrangement and try to water only the part where it is planted.

Rosette Types

Perle Von Nurnberg
Genus Echeveria. This is one of the most popular types of Echeveria, with attractive purple leaves. In spring it has small flowers. It is coated in a white powdery dusting.

Echeveria Pulidonis
Genus Echeveria. The green leaves are subtly tinged with red around the edges. Yellow flowers bloom in the spring.

Letizia
Genus Sedeveria. Characterized by its green color. The leaves gradually turn red as if they were burning when changing color.

Chihuahualinze
Genus Echeveria. There are claws at the ends of the leaves, which have a swollen look to them. The area around the claws is a red color.

Immediately catching the eye of anyone looking at an arrangement, this type is the model succulent. It is mainly seen in rosette form in the Echeveria genus in the Crassulaceae family. This attractive petal-like arrangement of leaves has won this plant many admirers, and for this reason, it has been hybridized and developed into many unusual varieties. The plants shown here are common varieties that TOKIIRO uses regularly, with the developed parent plant above and the offspring shown below. Quietly sending out more and more leaves as they grow, their beauty is there to be enjoyed as time passes.

Echeveria White Rose
Genus Echeveria. Formed from layers of thick whitish leaves with reddish tips, this plant closely resembles a pale green rose.

Echeveria Secunda
Genus Echeveria. The roundish leaves have a little reddish claw at their tip. The leaves form layers like a rose and become a more vivid green the more sunlight they receive.

Peacockii Princess Pearl
Genus Echeveria. Covered all over in a dusting of white powder, this plant has an aura of elegance. Its leaves are pointed at the tips and tinged slightly red around the claws.

Powder Blue
Genus Echeveria. The leaves have a bluish tone and faint red tinge around the edges. Dusted with a white coating, this plant is characterized by its translucent, subtle shading.

Haworthia Cuspidata
Genus Haworthia. The tips of the leaves are quite sharp. Triangular in shape, they fan out in a rosette formation.

Haworthia Cymbiformis Var Obtusa
Genus Haworthia. Small and spherical in form, this plant has leaves that appear full of water, creating a sense of viridescence.

Enjoying Haworthia

Haworthia Cooperi Var Truncata
Genus Haworthia. White veins stand out clearly against the green of the leaves, which are adorably plump and round.

Cymbiformis
Genus Haworthia. The leaves of this plant are large and slightly flat. Buds grow from the side of the main plant, blossoming with pink flowers in the spring. Grow in a well ventilated spot.

Obtusa
Genus Haworthia. Plump, petal-like leaves fan out to form a rosette shape as this plant grows. It likes dry conditions, so take care not to over water.

Haworthia Leightonii
Genus Haworthia. Turns a blackish purple in the fall. If it receives insufficient sunlight it tends to grow spindly (the stem becomes thin and unsteady and gaps between leaves become larger) so take care to prevent this.

Inhabiting the dimly lit spaces in the shadows cast by cliffs and tall trees, the Haworthia genus in the Liliaceae family have evolved to take in as much as possible of the tiny amounts of sunlight they receive. The tips of their leaves are translucent, giving them a mystical appearance. When they're in sunlight, the veins of the leaves clearly stand out, highlighting their translucency. These translucent segments are called "windows." Their size and form vary depending on the plant variety. Each time one looks at these succulents, one finds something to learn from their vitality and the evolutionary process that resulted in their windows.

Haworthia Turgida Var Pallidifolia
Genus Haworthia. This hybrid has fleshy, triangular, roly-poly semi-translucent leaves growing in layers, forming a cute shape. It grows best in a semi shaded spot outdoors where it is protected from rain.

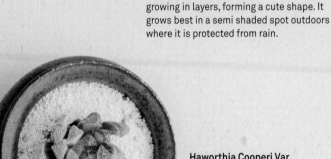

Haworthia Cooperi Var Pilifera Variegata
Genus Haworthia. Appearing white due its white dusting, even the veins in the leaves of this plant are transparent. Its long, narrow leaves grow upwards and spread out. It has white flowers.

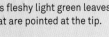

Haworthia Retusa (Var.)
Genus Haworthia. This plant has fleshy light green leaves that are pointed at the tip.

The Power of Vitality and Evolution

When we found this pot, we knew in a flash that we wanted to use it. But none of the succulents we considered planting in it were a match for the pot itself in terms of making a strong impression. A lot of time passed as the pot went unused—and then we found this Haworthia cooperi. It was the perfect combination: the green and white with the red and the plant with the pot struck just the right balance.

PLANTS USED
Cooperi (Genus Haworthia)

PLANTING TIP
When planting just one plant, prepare the container and pour the soil in the same way as outlined in Basic Methods for Planting on p10.

GROWING TIP
Although plants in the Genus Haworthia have evolved to be able to take in a lot of sunlight through their windows, they're unable to photosynthesize if continually in dark conditions. When the sun is shining softly, put them out to sunbathe. However, take care, as strong rays can cause the leaves to burn.

Container Garden 9
Celebrating Shadows

The reason we've planted succulents in glass containers is that we want you to look at the shadows that they cast. Whether they're blurred or clearly defined, all these shadows are beautiful.

PLANTS USED
1. Echeveria secunda (Genus Echeveria)
2. Pachyphytum oviferum (Genus Pachyphytum) Sedum rubrotinctum (Genus Sedum) Dragon's blood (Genus Sedum)
3. Sedum pachyphyllum (Genus Sedum) Pallidum (Genus Sedum)
4. Dragon's blood (Genus Sedum) Aurora (Genus Sedum)
5. Haworthia retusa (Genus Haworthia)
6. Echeveria sumirebotan (Genus Echeveria)

GROWING TIP
Place succulents on top of white sand. Do not water until they start putting out roots; begin watering once roots are showing.

Container Garden 10
The Gentleness of Pink

Container Garden 11
A Jewel on a Moonlit Night

We chose this round pot because it appears to cocoon the plant. The deliberately off-center positioning makes for a less constrained look.

Discovered in a jet black container, this jewel is the little child of Powder blue, which emits a calm blue light.

PLANTS USED
Perle von Nurnberg (Genus Echeveria)

PLANTING TIP
White ornamental sand has been used here. Carefully wash the salt off white Okinawan sand before strewing it over the surface of the soil. The white sand makes the pink of the succulent appear more saturated.

GROWING TIP
Leaves store water and sugar, so it's fine not to water too often. However, make sure plants receive plenty of sunlight.

PLANTS USED
Powder blue (Genus Echeveria)

PLANTING TIP
Plant in the same way as the Perle von Nurnberg on the left. After placing soil in the pot and planting in the Powder blue, white ornamental sand was strewn over the surface of the soil to complete the arrangement.

GROWING TIP
Place in a well ventilated area that receives good sunlight. This plant copes well with the cold, so even in winter it is best grown outdoors until the temperature drops below 37°F /3°C. When watering, give just enough to moisten the soil.

Mr Rabbit, What Did You
See That Made You Jump?

In the hollow of a snow-white fluffy cloud sits the full moon.
Are those rabbit footprints I see amid this quiet calm? What
can those rabbits have been playing at, I wonder?*

PLANTS USED
Kalanchoe eriophylla (Genus Kalanchoe)

PLANTING TIP
This arrangement is tied together with white—
white ornamental sand in a white container and
a white Kalanchoe eriophylla, which looks like
rabbit ears (hence its Japanese name of "Lucky
Rabbit Ear/s"). The image of playfully frolicking
white rabbits is one that brings happiness.

GROWING TIP
The white hairs on the leaves of Kalanchoe
eriophylla disappear if they get too much water,
so when watering, make sure to direct the
water onto the soil.

*Rabbits and the moon share a special
relationship in the East. The Japanese
version of the Man in the Moon is a rabbit
pounding rice cakes. Though his story
varies from country to country, he dwells
in the moon over China, Korea and
Vietnam as well.

The Flowers of Succulent Plants

Although there are individual differences, succulents do have flowers. Sadly, though, unlike other plants, they live in places with few birds or insects. Even if they want to send their descendants far away, there are no birds to carry them. So instead, they have evolved into attractive shapes and blossom for a long time so that someone—anyone at all—will find them. It's an evolutionary survival tactic.

If succulents are kept indoors where bright lights are on at night, they won't bloom. Please put them outdoors where it is dark. Succulents need to experience the change of light from day to night.

Container Garden 13
Memory

Thinking back to old memories, things become simple. Clear forms are out of reach and only fuzzy silhouettes remain. Colors are the same—they fade, leaving a mono-tone view of the world.

PLANTS USED
Echeveria pulvinata "frosty" (Genus Echeveria)
Crassula lycopodioides (Genus Crassulaceae)
Echeveria sumirebotan (Genus Echeveria)
Sedum Alice Evans (Genus Sedum)

PLANTING TIP
"Frosty," planted in the center, is covered in hair and looks white, making the image of faded color even stronger. There's the whitish succulent of the sumirebotan; Crassula lycopodioides has beautiful greenery all year round and Sedum Alice Evans has white flowers.

GROWING TIP
When planting, leave some space around each plant. This allows each plant to receive enough light and water.

Container Garden 14
Quietly Listening to the Voices of Plants

Why are you a certain shape? Why are you a certain color? Try to see things from a succulent's perspective and listen to what they're saying: these plants that have evolved so slowly over time will start telling you about their history.

PLANTS USED
Echeveria white rose (Genus Echeveria)
Echeveria domingo (Genus Echeveria)
Crassula salmentosa (Genus Crassulaceae)
Aeonium undulatum (Genus Aeonium)

PLANTING TIP
The "Memory" on the left is created to conjure the image of a city. Conversely, to bring the image of a forest to mind in this arrangement, we planted the succulents together densely. It's a wild look, with plants doing as they please.

GROWING TIP
To bring out plants' inherent wildness, don't fuss over their maintenance too much, but at the same time, don't forget to check on them daily.

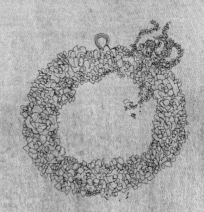

Chapter

2

Using Succulents to Add Color to Walls
Creating Wreaths and Tableaux

Tokiiro had its start with wreaths made from succulents. Guided by the first wreath we made, succulents have become our life's work. If we hadn't had that encounter with the wreath, Tokiiro would never have come into existence. We treasure these wreaths and sincerely hope you will create them too. They are "living wreaths"—capturing the shift between seasons, they change from green to red, red to green as time passes, as only a wreath made from succulents can. It's something special that is possible only because the plants are alive. We hope you'll enjoy them all year round.

Succulents for Wreaths

Wreaths are usually meant for hanging, so making sure nothing can fall out of the arrangement is an ironclad rule. For this reason, select succulents with stems that are thick and sturdy. Check the condition of the stems as you prepare them as per the photos. Don't they look sweet all lined up together like this? Even succulents of the same type each have their own different expressions, so consider their individual looks as you choose which ones to use.

Succulents Suitable for Wreaths

Echeveria White Rose

Genus Echeveria. Fleshy with a white tinge and pink around the tips of the leaves. They love light, so make sure they get plenty of sun. Insufficient light makes them spindly and unattractive.

Snow

Genus Sedeveria. Leaves are long and thin with a roundness to them and develop a pink tinge at the tips. They do not cope well with heat so care is needed in midsummer, and they should be moved to a cool spot. Have large and small specimens on hand to combine in arrangements.

Sedum Rubrotinctum

Genus Sedum. The glossy, chubby leaves are cute, and change color depending on the season, so enjoy the gradation this creates. They tend to grow towards light, so make sure it falls around them evenly.

Sedum Pachyphyllum

Genus Sedum. Only the tips of the leaves change color, turning pink. Any damages to the stems weaken the plant, so when removing lower leaves, handle carefully to avoid damage.

How to Make a Succulent Wreath
Using Succulents to Add Color to Walls

Besides being a ring of flowers or greens, a wreath is a symbol of eternity and immortality. The neat, round form of a wreath has no end. It's a bit of everlasting happiness. Let's create that out of succulents. Depending on the time of year, the wreath will be green or will turn red, allowing you to feel the never-ending connection of the seasons.

Basic Tools for Making Wreaths

Tokiiro's style is to plant succulents in a wreath base in such a way that they'll go on living forever. In order for these plants to live, there must be soil in the wreath base. The succulents must be allowed to take root in this soil. Roots should start to appear in about a month.

1 Screwdrivers (thick, medium, fine)

When planting succulents in the wreath base, use these to make holes in the base and then insert the plants. Have screwdrivers in three different thicknesses to match the various stem thicknesses of the plants. When making the wreath, the soil is packed in hard and firm, so if you don't have a screwdriver some other kind of metal skewer that can withstand the soil will be fine.

2 Sphagnum Moss

Sphagnum moss is used to cover the surface of the wreath base, as well as to stabilize the plants within it and prevent soil from spilling out of it. It can be purchased at a home center.

3 Scissors

Use to trim off the lower leaves from the succulents to be planted in the wreath base. This makes it easier to insert the stems in to the base.

4 Pliers

Use to mend and alter the metal mesh used to make the wreath base, bending wire into wall hooks, and so on.

5 Wire

Use for making into wall hooks. Have a length of #24 florist's wire on hand.

6 Tweezers

Use to insert sphagnum moss into the wreath base. Again, the type with bent tips is recommended as they make detailed work easier.

7 Wreath Base

Instructions for making the wreath base are on p50–52. For the succulents to develop comfortably, soil is a key component. This applies to all planting, whether in containers or in wreaths. Make sure the plants take root and that they're able to absorb water, nutrients and so on.

1. Create the Wreath Base

As just mentioned, you will be putting soil into the wreath base. However, your work will be for nothing if the soil falls out when the wreath is hanging on a wall. The soil must be firmly covered with sphagnum moss and mesh to prevent it from spilling out. This wreath base construction forms the foundation for a beautiful wreath.

Materials and equipment (for one wreath 5 inches [12 cm] in diameter)

1. Pliers
2. Scissors
3. Florist's wire #24: eight pieces, each 2 inches (5 cm) long
4. Scoop
5. Soil
6. Tray x 2 (with one side longer than 13.5 inches [34 cm])
7. Sphagnum moss
8. Wire mesh (13.5 x 4 inches [34 x 10 cm])
9. Doweling (⅞ inches [2 cm] diameter, 13¾–15¾ inches [35 x 40 cm] long)

Create a Sheet of Sphagnum Moss

Lay out plenty of sphagnum moss on tray.

Place another tray on top.

Keeping the trays together, turn upside down and place a weight on top. Leave overnight.

The completed sheet.

Create the Outer Shell for the Wreath (Sphagnum Moss Net)

Turn up the edge of the long side of the wire mesh.

Place the sphagnum moss sheet on top of the mesh and cut it to the size of the mesh. Bend the other edge of the wire mesh over to hold the sheet in place.

The mesh should now look like this.

Form It Into a Cylinder

Place the doweling on top of the sphagnum moss sheet and roll the edges in as you would a sushi roll. Remove the doweling and make sure there are no holes.

If there are any, use your hands to add sphagnum moss to fill them in. Add soil inside moss. Press the soil in with your hands.

Cover the edges with sphagnum moss so the soil doesn't fall out.

Bring the two edges together, overlapping slightly. The entire cylinder should be covered with sphagnum moss so the soil isn't visible.

Use pliers to twist the edges of the wire mesh together into the wreath base and secure it in place. Trim the edges of the wire after securing.

Press more sphagnum moss into places where the black soil is visible.

Thread wire in through places where the mesh joins and secure so mesh will not open out. Do this in about 5–6 places, about 2 inches (5 cm) apart.

Trim off excess wire and poke edges into wreath base so it is no longer visible. Cover one end of the rod-shaped net with mesh to close it off.

Use pliers to open out the mesh at the other end.

Bend the rod-shaped net into a circle and join the ends together.

Run two pieces of wire through the sections above and below the joins to keep the circle in place.

Create a Wall Hook

Twist a fine piece of wire into a ring shape. With the ring section on the outer edge, wrap the wire around the wreath base.

Trim off excess wire and neaten.

The completed wreath base. This is what the succulents will be planted in.

2. Prepare the Succulents

The succulents needed for this wreath are listed on p44–47. In order to make it easy to work them into the wreath, round out the foliage and neaten the stems. If the removed leaves are placed on soil as shown on p25, they'll start to put out roots and buds in about a month's time and continue to live and grow.

Brush off excess soil and trim roots.

Remove excess leaves so that foliage forms a round shape.

Trim stems to about $^7/_8$–$1^1/_8$ inches (2–3 cm) long.

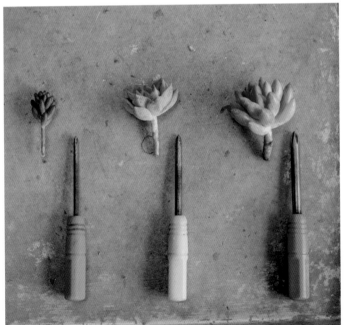

LEFT Stems should be the length of the wreath's base. In the case of this wreath, which has a base $1^1/_8$ inches (3 cm) thick, the stems should ideally be about $^7/_8$–$1^1/_8$ inches (2–3 cm) long. It's helpful to have screwdrivers of different thicknesses at hand to match the thicknesses of the stems.

ABOVE A "tray" of mesh wrapped over a shallow box or deep tray makes it easier to organize succulents. It also reduces the stress on the plants, so is like killing two birds with one stone.

3. Planting the Succulents in the Wreath Base

Put simply, this task involves making holes in the wreath base and planting the succulents in the holes, securing them so they don't fall out. Securing them into place is the tricky part. Use the side of the screwdriver blade to press in the sphagnum moss and soil surrounding the plants' stems from all directions. Do this thoroughly, without rushing.

Planting the Succulents

Make a hole with the screwdriver. The soil is packed in firmly in the wreath base, so this requires a bit of strength.

Place the succulent in the hole.

If the stem of the succulent is long, use scissors to trim it until the plant can sit with the leaves flush against the wreath base. This is how it should look.

Securing the Succulents in Place

Work the screwdriver in from an adjoining hole in the mesh and use the side of it to press sphagnum moss and soil around the stem of the plant. Do this all around the stem, pressing it in firmly from every direction until the plant is fully secured.

Work in sphagnum moss to fill in any holes that may have formed around the stem so that the soil isn't visible.

A surprising amount of sphagnum moss is necessary. Even amounts that appear excessive turn out to be just right, as the moss becomes concentrated when compacted.

Balance the Wreath with Three "Accent" Succulents

Create an attractive balance by first placing three large "accent" plants and then planting other small succulents in between them to fill in the spaces. Plant them all in the same way as on the page at the left, using screwdrivers the same thickness as the stems to make holes to put the plants in, leaving no gaps. Fill in any holes made when securing the stems by working in sphagnum moss before planting the next plant. The key to an attractive result is to complete each task thoroughly. If the sphagnum moss in the wreath base is visible, it ruins the overall look of the wreath, so it's also important to plant the succulents so that the base is completely covered when seen from the front.

4. Turn the Wreath Upside Down and Fill in Any Holes with Sphagnum Moss

Fill in holes using sphagnum moss as shown on p54. Make sure to work the moss in thoroughly to get rid of the visible sections of black soil and prevent soil from falling out of the wreath.

Turn over and check thoroughly.

Viewed from the side.

HOW TO WATER THE WREATH

As when planting in a container, plants undergo a stress period right after the wreath is made. Leave it to rest undisturbed so the plants can settle into their new environment. If watered at this time they'll lose their vitality, so care is needed. Leave the wreath undisturbed for around three weeks, then check its appearance before watering. Water the wreath by placing it in a bowl and spraying it with a shower hose from above. Once the entire wreath is covered in water, leave it there for 15 minutes. The next watering depends on the plants' condition, but aim for about two weeks later. Check the plants daily and if they seem thirsty, give them some water. By monitoring them daily and caring for them you will get a feel for what the plants need.

Place the wreath in a large bowl and use a sprayer to add water.

Once the water fills up the bowl, leave the wreath to sit for 15 minutes.

Wreath 1
Seasonal Color

The wreath is complete. The red succulents are sporting their fall colors. This red will change to green in spring as it gets warmer and the sun's rays increase. The red returns in the fall as the temperature drops and the sun's rays weaken, but because the wreath is alive and dynamic, it still looks different from year to year.

Wreath 2

Tranquil Eternity

Colors are kept simple and subtle in this white and green wreath, which gives off a quiet air of relaxed sophistication. Here is a simple, enduring vitality that remains unchanged despite the passing of time.

PLANTING TIP
The number of types that change color has been reduced in this arrangement. Succulents that turn vivid shades are inevitably seen as cute, so this has been slightly toned down to create a more grown up look. Other succulents change relatively little with the seasons, so this aspect is played up here.

GROWING TIP
Water as per p56. Make sure to immerse thoroughly.

Commonly known as air plants, plants in the genus Tillandsia are also succulents. This wreath consists entirely of Tillandsia. Able to withstand extremes in heat and humidity, the resilient plants used here can live anywhere as long as they get light.

Wreath 3

The World's Most Enduring Greenery

PLANTS USED
Tillandsia usneoides
(Family Bromeliad,
Genus Ttillandsia)
Tillandsia lonantha
(Family Bromeliad,
Genus Tillandsia)

PLANTING TIP
The base is a store-bought wreath made from woody vines. Masses of usneoides threads are placed over it, neatened and fastened into place with 0.3mm brass wire. For instructions, see step 2. (Attaching the Air Plants) on p63.

GROWING TIP
As long as sunlight can get in and it is bright enough, even the window frame of a bathroom makes an interesting spot to grow this wreath. Of course it does OK indoors, but this is a plant that has evolved to grow along the branches of large trees, so it will be happiest if it receives plenty of water and fresh air.

How would it be possible to use succulents as an accent in an arrangement and keep them alive? Pondering this question, we came up with this. Doesn't it look exactly like the wreath is wearing a corsage?

Wreath 4
Just Like a Corsage

PLANTS USED
Bartramii (Genus Graptopetalum)
Aeonium domesticum (Genus Aeonium)
Senecio rowleyanus (Family Asteraceae, Genus Senecio)
Silver pet (Genus Sedum)
Crassula expansa (Genus Crassulaceae)
Sedum rubrotinctum (Genus Sedum)
Graptopetalum bronze (Genus Graptopetalum)
Tillandsia usneoides (Family Bromeliad, Genus Tillandsia)

PLANTING TIP
The defining characteristic of this store-bought wreath covered in Tillandsia is the soil added to a section of the wreath base to ensure the succulents stay alive. Detailed instructions for making it are on p62–63. Many succulents live together in this small space.

Wreaths Made with Air Plants
Variations

As a variation on the wreath, we tried using air plants. The wreath on page 60 is made solely from air plants, while the wreath on page 61 combines air plants and other succulents. The official name of this plant is Tillandsia usneoides. It is also called Spanish moss. It can live without soil, so a wreath of air plants can be made simply by winding the plants around a store-bought wreath. For a combined wreath, sections with succulents will need to include soil.

1. Make the Air Plant Wreath Base

A store-bought wreath is used for the section with the air plants, while the wreath base outlined on p50–52 is used for the succulents. A combination of these two is used for the wreath shown here.

For a section with succulents...

Follow the directions for making a wreath base on p50–52, however only make a very short section. And when packing the soil in, add a thick piece of wire so this part can be attached to the store-bought wreath.

Materials and equipment
1. Garden Shear
2. Scissors
3. Construction Wire
4. 0.3mm Brass Wire
5. Florist's Wire #24
6. Base in which to plant succulents (see above)
7. Spanish moss (Tillandsia usneoides Family Bromeliad)
8. Store-bought Wreath (made from vines)

Place the base for the succulents made from sphagnum moss against the store-bought wreath to check the size. Wind wire around the store-bought wreath to hold it at the left and right of the section where the succulent base will be slotted in.

Use shears to cut out the section where the succulent base will be added. Slot the succulent base into the cut-out section.

To secure the joints of the wreath and succulent base, tie two pieces of construction wire at the outer and inner edges of the wreath on both sides and join the sections together firmly.

2. Attaching the Air Plants

Once the wreath base is ready, add Spanish moss using fine brass wire. We've found that this type of wire is the least obtrusive and gives the neatest result.

Spread air plants lightly over store-bought wreath base so the base can no longer be seen.

Use 0.3mm brass wire to fasten air plants to the store-bought wreath base in about eight places, checking the effect as you work.

3. Add Succulents to the Wreath

Use the same method given on p54 to add succulents to the section of the wreath you've added for them. The result is shown on p61. Beautiful!

How to Make a Tableau Wall Hanging

A "tableau" is the French term for a wall hanging. At Tokiiro we make name plaques, message boards and so on that incorporate succulents. Even the smallest amount of green adds a touch of chic to any room and has a healing effect on those viewing it. Although small, its effects are significant!

Basic Equipment and Materials for Creating Tableaux

The equipment needed for creating tableaux is basically the same as that needed for creating wreaths. The only difference is that a tableau base is used. This can be square, round, or whatever shape you like, so try making various tweaks to get the desired result. Here, we are using a basic rectangular base. Create a section at the edge of the board to plant the succulents, with blank space left for writing something such as a message.

1 Sphagnum Moss
Use this to create a soil base for the section where the succulents will be planted. Handle it in the same way as you would when creating a wreath. The aim is to cover soil to prevent it spilling out.

2 Tableau Base
For the tableau base, use a board in your preferred size, painted whatever color you like, with a hole cut out. The base in the photo is 3½ x 8 inches (8 x 20 cm) and the hole is 1 inch (2.5 cm) in diameter.

3 Wire Mesh (3¼ x 3¼ inches [8 x 8 cm])
Use the same type as is used to create wreath bases.

4 Tweezers
Use to plant succulents, reinforce sphagnum moss and so on.

5 Doweling
Use to roll wire mesh into a cylinder, to compress sphagnum moss and water and so on.

6 Scissors
Use to cut wire mesh to a suitable size.

7 Pliers
Use to bend back the loose ends of wire mesh.

1. Create the Tableau Base

The tableau essentially uses the same methods as those for creating wreaths. As for a wreath, create a sphagnum moss net, then roll it into a ball. Press it into the hole in the tableau base and plant succulents into it.

Press a large doweling or brown handle into the wire mesh and round it out to the size of the hole in your base.

Cut to about 2 inches (5 cm) long and trim off the excess with scissors.

Open out the wire mesh and line it with sphagnum moss.

Use the doweling to press the sphagnum moss and compact it inside the mesh.

After doweling is removed, the moss should form a solid sheath inside wire mesh.

Pour in the soil and use the doweling to compact the soil down.

Cover the soil with sphagnum moss so it is no longer visible.

Use pliers to bend the edges of the wire mesh around the sphagnum moss to form a ball shape.

The moss worked into a ball.

Place the ball of moss into the hole in the tableau base.

Press ball from behind to flatten it and make it flush with the back of the board. This means it will sit flat when it is hung on a wall and will not fall out.

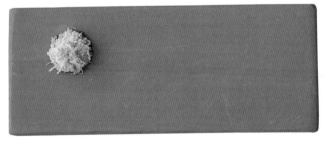

Space has been left to write messages, names and so on, but if you get rid of the message space and increase the size of the section in which to plant succulents, the board can be made into a frame of succulents (see p69).

2. Preparing the Succulents

Line up your choice of succulents on a tray. The succulents to use are the same as those for the wreath (see p44) but adding a little movement makes the arrangement more interesting, so here we've added some "trailing succulents" (see p72).

1 Sedum mexicanum (Genus Sedum)
2 Echeveria white rose (Genus Echeveria)
3 Silver pet (Genus Sedum)
4 Echeveria mini bell (Genus Echeveria)
5 Sedum spurium cv Tricolor (Genus Sedum)
6 Sedum adolphi (Genus Sedum)

7 Sedum rubrotinctum (Genus Sedum)
8 Sedum pachyphyllum (Genus Sedum)
9 Bartramii (Genus Graptopetalum)
10 Aeonium domesticum (Genus Aeonium)
11 Senecio rowleyanus (Family Asteraceae, Genus Senecio)

3. Planting the Succulents in the Ball

The basic planting technique is the same as for the wreath, but this arrangement uses trailing plants, so plant them in first.

Prepare the length of Senecio rowleyanus you want to use as the trailing succulent in the arrangement and consider the overall balance of the composition.

Use a screwdriver to create a hole in the ball and insert the roots of Senecio rowleyanus into the hole. The roots and stem are soft, so plant using tweezers for a neat finish.

Position the Senecio rowleyanus around the ball and secure in place with mini U pins. Use U pins that are smaller than the width of the tableau base for an attractive finish, working them into the ball section in about two different places to secure the plant.

Plant the other plants into the ball as per the wreath. Begin with the larger eye catching succulents and then work smaller ones in to cover the ball.

Tableau 1

A Pop-out Picture

The tableau differs from the wreath in that the succulents hang out beyond the frame. It's a living picture, whimsical and novel. If it is hung on a wall for an extended period, each plant in the tableau tends to grow towards the sun. Sedum rubrotinctum responds quickly and its capacity for sun-following can't be surpassed. The other plants do as they please, some growing vertically while others trail down. All this natural activity plays out in this small space, highlighting the inherent natural power in each plant.

Tableau 2

An old clock turned into a tableau with soil poured into the backing of the clock.

Tableau 3

This frame of succulents has been created by removing a large section from the center of a board and planting it with succulents.

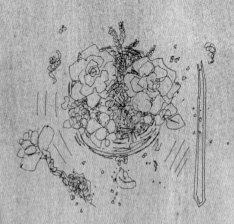

Chapter

3

Floating in the Air
Hanging Succulents

These hanging succulents leap out from their
containers as if floating in mid-air. They look
like green airships on a journey into space!
Plant them with the thought of opening up
new horizons as you gaze at them.

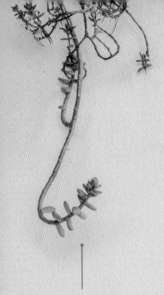

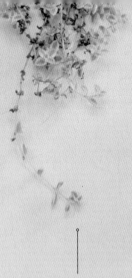

Little Missy
Genus Crassulaceae. Over
time this plant trails further
and further down as it grows.
It likes dry conditions.

ABOVE **Punctulata**

BELOW **Sedum Oaxacanum**
Punctulata belongs to the genus
Crassulaceae. They're characterized by their leaves, which grow
crucifix-style. Oaxacanum is part
of the genus Sedum. The leaves
grow radially around the stem and
they have white flowers.

Crassula Marnieriana
Genus Crassulaceae. It actually
grows vertically, but after a
while begins to trail down. The
square leaves appear to be
stacked one on top of the other
but closer inspection shows
that they grow in alternating
cross formations.

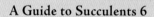

A Guide to Succulents 6

Succulents That are Ideal for Hanging

Senecio rowleyanus, Othonna capensis and so on from the
Asteraceae family are typical examples of trailing plants.
Hanging arrangements are meant to be enjoyed for the world
they evoke as they spill out of the container, rather than to be
closely scrutinized for what the container holds, and as such,
the Asteraceae are ideal for this purpose. Other plants used
here have actually been trained to hang down, the cherished
results of months and years of work.

Sedum Morganianum
Genus Sedum. This plant never stands erect. It thrives in high humidity but is vulnerable to cold, and may freeze if placed outside in winter. Covering it in plastic to create an impromptu greenhouse is an effective measure against cold.

Senecio Rowleyanus
Family Asteraceae, Genus Senecio. A member of the Asteraceae family, like the Othonna Capensis, it loves water. However, it is a different genus, and this shows in its flowers. It is a fast grower.

Othonna Capensis
Family Asteraceae, Genus Othonna. Plants in the Asteraceae family love water, so if you plant them in an arrangement with succulents that like dry conditions, make sure to give only the section in which they're planted plenty of water.

Hanging Garden 1
A Forgotten Forest

On page 93 we write about environmental changes and how the inherent power of nature takes over with such strength in places from which people have become absent, turning them into a paradise for plants. This is what we've tried to express here—succulents continuing to generate life from inside the iron relics.

PLANTS USED
Sedum mexicanum (Genus Sedum)
Sedum morganianum (Genus Sedum)
Sedum Alice Evans (Genus Sedum)
Sedum rubrotinctum (Genus Sedum)
Graptopetalum bronze (Genus Graptopetalum)
Echeveria white rose (Genus Echeveria)
Snow (Genus Sedeveria)
Sedum adolphi (Genus Sedum)
Sedum makinoi (Genus Sedum)
Senecio rowleyanus (Family Asteraceae, Genus Senecio)
Crassula salmentosa (Genus Crassulaceae)
Graptopetalum paraguayense (Genus Graptopetalum)
Momiji matsuri (Genus Crassulaceae)

PLANTING AND GROWING TIP
Here, it is as if untouched nature has been planted and is being cultivated. Succulents that want to reach upwards grow vertically, while those that want to hang down do just that. When a strong succulent is next to a weak one, the weak succulent may give up its place to the strong one. That's the way of nature, and it's acknowledged in this arrangement.

Prepare the Container for Hanging

Whether you set your container on a flat surface or suspend it in the air, the planting technique is essentially the same, so here we focus on preparing containers for hanging, both from overhead and from a wall.

1. Creating a Container to Hang from the Ceiling

The finished item. The length of the hanging wire is up to you.

Materials/equipment: pliers, container, mesh for base, wire. Drill a hole in the container as shown on p10.

Bend one end of a piece of wire 90 degrees.

Bend the wire into a square to fit underneath of the container base.

After making three bends, make a shorter fourth bend, then a fifth bend so the long end of the wire can pass up through the hole in the base of the container.

Pass the long end of the unbent section of wire through the hole in the base of the container.

Turn the container so the base faces down and pass the center of the mesh over the wire.

Bend the end of the wire into a J shape to form a hook.

Type that hangs overhead.

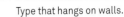
Type that hangs on walls.

2. Creating a Container to Hang on a Wall

The finished item.

Materials/equipment: pliers, container, mesh for base, wire, electric drill.

Drill two holes in the side of the container, each equidistant from the rim. Start with a fine drill bit, gradually increasing until the holes are wide enough for the wire to pass through.

Bend the wire into a U shape matching the distance between the holes. Decide on the length of the wall hook.

Hold the wire against the container as it will look when finished and bend both ends at a 90-degree angle, making sure your ends will be long enough to bend up and wrap around your hanger wire. Working from inside the container, pass the ends of the bent wire through the holes.

Bend the wire ends up and over the container rim.

Wrap the ends around the hanger wire securely and trim any excess.

PLANTS USED

ABOVE LEFT
Echeveria runyonii (Genus Echeveria)
Little missy (Genus Crassulaceae)
Acre aureum (Genus Sedum)
Punctulata (Genus Crassulaceae)
Momiji matsuri (Genus Crassulaceae)
Perle von Nurnberg (Genus Echeveria)
Senecio rowleyanus (Family Asteraceae, Genus Senecio)

ABOVE RIGHT
Echeveria white rose (Genus Echeveria)
Makinoi ogon (Genus Sedum)
Sedum makinoi (Genus Sedum)
Acre aureum (Genus Sedum)

OPPOSITE
Crassula lycopodioides (Genus Crassulaceae)
Senecio rowleyanus (Family Asteraceae, Genus Senecio)
Little missy (Genus Crassulaceae)
Sedeveria silver frost (Genus Sedeveria)
Dragon's blood (Genus Sedum)
Sedum spurium cv tricolor (Genus Sedum)
Sedum adolphi (Genus Sedum)
Silver pet (Genus Sedum)

PLANTING TIP
Senecio rowleyanus and other trailing types of succulent are planted in the very center of the container. If there are plenty of places where they're in direct contact with the soil, they'll put roots out and secure themselves firmly in the ground.

GROWING TIP
Hanging the containers in the air prevents an influx of ants. Good ventilation is another plus. When watering, check plants' condition and give them plenty of water as per the instructions for containers on p25.

Hanging Garden 2

Three Spacecraft Flying Through the Air

A spaceship loaded with trailing plants
A spaceship with a few plants trailing from it
A round, compact spaceship
Which one will you ride in?

Leaving Home

The simpler the container, the more eye-catching are the succulents leaping out of it. Where's that one going that's jumping out of its container home? Changing your perspective reveals different viewpoints and personalities in the plants.

PLANTS USED
Echeveria pulidonis (Genus Echeveria)
Crassula marnieriana (Genus Crassulaceae)
Punctulata (Genus Crassulaceae)
Little missy (Genus Crassulaceae)
Aurora (Genus Sedum)
Acre aureum (Genus Sedum)
Sedum spurium cv tricolor (Genus Sedum)

PLANTING TIP
Starting with Crassula marnieriana which plays the leading role, consider the silhouette of the arrangement in order to work out positions for planting.

GROWING TIP
Immediately after being planted is an unnatural time for plants. They'll be stressed in their new environment, so wait a week before watering them (refer to the watering schedule on p25). After a month, each succulent will display its natural characteristics and bring forth the beauty of nature.

Chapter

4

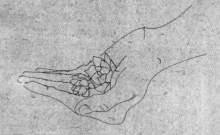

Living with Succulents

Up to this point, we've discussed various aspects of
arranging succulents. In this chapter we'll discuss the
things you should know in order to care for and live
with succulents. Always remember that succulents are
living things, so as you gather info, keep the plants'
perspective in mind. What kind of environments have
succulents survived in up until now? Taking a look even
at this single aspect will give us insights into the souls of
succulents.

What is a Succulent?

While "succulent" is just one word, types of succulent number in the thousands. However, what they all have in common is that they store water in their leaves, stems or inside their roots. The general term for plants that do this is "succulent." TOKIIRO tends to handle succulents that store water and nutrients mainly in their leaves such as some of those in the families Crassulaceae, Asteraceae and Liliaceae. Cacti typify those that store water in their stems, while caudiciforms are representative of those that store it in their roots.

Succulents originate mainly from arid regions such as the deserts and coastlines of Latin America and South Africa. Imagine what these places are like—during the day, the sun is fierce, and there is little moisture so the air is as dry as a bone. At night, temperatures drop dramatically, with a difference in day to night temperatures of as much as 104°F/40°C. Plants have evolved to be able to live resiliently in such conditions by taking in moisture to store inside their structures and drawing on it in order to live. During the heat of the day, they close the pores (openings that act as mouths for plants) in their leaves to avoid moisture from inside their structures evaporating, while in the cool of the night they open their pores to allow them to regulate their temperature. Therefore, there are lots of succulents that can't cope well with the hot, humid nights.

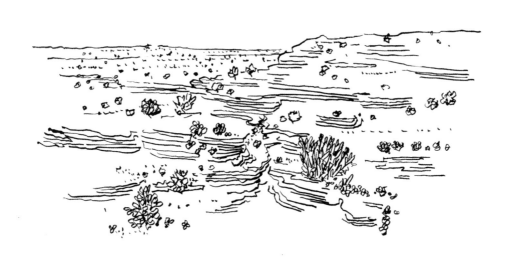

Succulents Love Water!

Once you hear that succulents' natural habitat is deserts and arid regions, you probably think they like hot places and don't need much water at all.

However, in actual fact, succulents love water. As mentioned previously, succulents came to grow in arid environments with strong sunlight and over a long stretch of time they have evolved to suit these surroundings, storing water in their structures, developing unique forms and colors and so on. This is why the way they grow and how they propagate have also come to differ from other plants. As they have evolved to keep up with the changes to the earth's environment, I believe that they'll continue their process of evolution.

Photosynthesis Prompts a Love of Water

We've noted that succulents love water, as it allows them to carry out photosynthesis. All plants, not just succulents, perform photosynthesis. Maybe you didn't do so well in this subject in middle school, but don't close the book—please keep reading!

Photosynthesis is a biological activity, as are breathing, drawing nutrients from food and turning those nutrients into energy for humans. Plants breathe and convert sugars (nutrients) into energy to support life. To do this, they need three elements: carbon dioxide, water and sunlight. Carbon dioxide is absorbed into the body of the plant and in response, the plant creates oxygen, water and nutritional sugars. In chemical terms, this process is: $6\,CO_2 + 12\,H_2O \rightarrow C_6H_{12}O_6 + 6\,H_2O + 6\,O_2$.

The oxygen created is expelled into the atmosphere via the pores in the plant. If you look at modern buildings with greenery incorporated into the walls and gardens installed throughout the stories, it's clear that harmony with nature is being fostered as part of city planning. But is it only for the benefit of humans?

Growing greenery on buildings is an attempt to convert carbon dioxide, one of the gases in the atmosphere that causes global warming, into oxygen. From the plants' perspective, carbon dioxide is vital for survival. So for all our sakes, it's important for each of us to make even a small effort to enable photosynthesis.

Succulents store water internally, and if given too much from external sources, a detrimental excess will result. Because of this, it's easy to think that watering succulents isn't necessary. But while they need far less than other types of plants, succulents do still need water.

Creating an Environment to Promote Photosynthesis

The speed at which photosynthesis occurs depends of course on the strength of sunlight, with the density of carbon dioxide, temperature and so on also having a major influence. Generally, photosynthesis is activated between in temperatures of 50–85°F/ 10–30°C. Chlorophyll, the pigment that causes leaves to be green, is also actively stimulated, but outside of this temperature range photosynthesis radically slows and chlorophyll gradually breaks down. Similarly, photosynthesis is impeded if there is an imbalance of water, carbon dioxide or sunlight—that is, if any of these are significantly lacking.

When this happens, the plant attempts to transform in pursuit of the lacking element. For example, insufficient sunlight will cause a plant to grow long and spindly as it seeks light, while a lack of water will cause it to use up its internal water stores. When a plant receives insufficient water, it cannot circulate the sugars created during photosynthesis or the essential elements absorbed through the roots. Once its internal stores of water are used up, the plant withers. Given the earth's environment, it's hard to imagine supplies of carbon dioxide becoming scarce, but if it were to happen, the ecosystem would not be able to exist and plants would wither and die.

In winter seasons below 50°F/10°C and summer seasons above 85°F/30°C the temperature restricts photosynthesis. For this reason, it's fine to replenish water only minimally. During times when photosynthesis is limited, succulents draw on their reserves of nutrients in order to maintain their vitality.

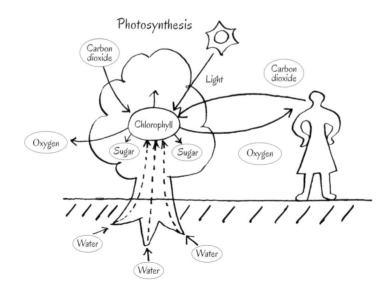

Photosynthesis in Succulents Differs from That in Other Plants

Having adapted and evolved over many years to suit the climate and environment of their habitat, succulents have also evolved their method of photosynthesis to match their surroundings. This particular method, or carbon fixation pathway, is called Crassulacean Acid Metabolism (CAM) photosynthesis. Most plants absorb carbon dioxide during the day and create sugars through photosynthesis, releasing oxygen. However, in the case of succulents, photosynthesis begins at night.

To prevent themselves from drying out, during the heat of the day succulents close the pores which allow the passing of carbon dioxide and oxygen, thereby minimizing the loss of moisture. In the cool of the night, they open their pores to take in carbon dioxide, storing this nourishment as malic acid in their vacuoles until daytime, when they use the reaction of malic acid and light to produce sugar (glucose). This process is CAM photosynthesis. It is thought that development of succulents is slow due to the large amount of time and energy involved in this photosynthesis.

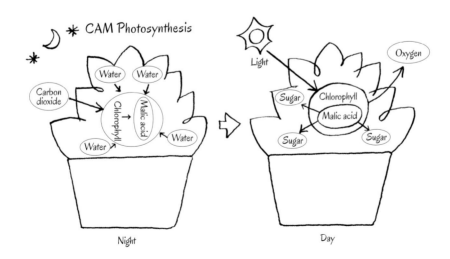

CAM Photosynthesis

Night

Day

Succulents are Not Good Indoor Dwellers

Succulents take in carbon dioxide at night, so it makes sense that being placed in an enclosed space overnight causes them stress. Unable to breathe adequately, they cannot create nourishment and will thus become weak, causing a build-up of stress and leading to the plant suffering unbearably. Therefore, as much as possible, at night as well as during the day, place succulents in a spot where air circulates well. This is a good environment for succulents.

"An enclosed space overnight" basically means indoors, so make sure to keep that in mind. Succulents are not indoor greenery!

Although succulents are shown more and more as interior objects in lifestyle magazines and so on, most of them have evolved to thrive in environments with harsh sun. For plants such as these, the amount of light indoors is nowhere near sufficient and survival becomes difficult.

Light, Air and Water are Vital for Succulents

Having said that, it is difficult to recreate the environment in which succulents grow naturally. If you're caring for them outdoors, airflow should not be a problem. However, air is not the only thing succulents require to grow happily.

Light, air and water—these three basics are essential to a succulent's longevity. It's that simple. Additionally, rather than looking at things from a human perspective in terms of where to place them, consider things from the plant's viewpoint as to where it would like to live.

Check in daily with your plants as to where they'd like to be, whether they have enough water, whether they're getting enough light and air and so on. By doing this, you'll gradually be able to hear plants' voices and understand what it is that they want.

The Charm of Succulents

Why do we enjoy succulents do much? It's because of their shape and color, their vitality and their ability to adapt to their environment that have so charmed us.

The first time we saw succulents, we were thrilled by their individuality. We remember talking to them, saying things like, "what a wonderful form you have… you're truly alive, aren't you?" Researching them, we discovered such an abundance of varieties, all with their own charming shapes and colors, that we became more and more captivated by them. As we spent time with them, we found there were many moving moments to be had and discoveries to be made. For example, new shoots grow from a single leaf; the bare stalk of a plant that we were so disappointed about was actually growing sweet offspring!

Why are shoots sprouting? Why do they have these particular shapes? Why are they so colorful? Why are they growing hairs?

We came up with more and more questions about succulents and wanted to learn more about them.

We learned that succulents live in unforgiving environments and have evolved slowly in order to survive, changing to adapt to their conditions, persisting with their appearance, form and color to ensure their survival.

For example, it's believed that the Haworthia genus of the Liliaeceae family evolved in the shadows of large cliffs and trees and developed transparent sections at the tips of their leaves to maximize what little light reached them. The eriophylla (see p18) with its rabbit ear-like leaves, and others in the Kalanchoe family, are covered in hair to control the amount of sunlight that reaches their leaves. Similarly, some types of plants in the Echeveria genus control the amount of sunlight they receive by means of a powdery substance that covers their leaves.

The Beauty of Succulents' Fall Colors

Certain succulents change color in the fall. Of course these succulents originated in South America, South Africa and so on, but since succulents were introduced to other parts of the world, many producers have bred to suit the local climate. In some cases, this process goes back two hundred years.

There are two types of color transformation—yellow and red. Plants have a yellow pigment in their leaves called carotenoid. In seasons where photosynthesis is occurring at a great rate, large stocks of pigment that appears green (chlorophyll) are produced via photosynthesis and carotenoid becomes concealed. However, once the temperature drops and photosynthetic activity decreases, the production of chlorophyll also decreases and under the influence of the inherent yellow pigment of the carotenoid, the plant turns yellow.

So, why do plants change color? When the temperature drops and photosynthesis decreases, the sugars stored in plants' leaves react to the ultraviolet rays from the sun to produce a red pigment called anthocyanin, resulting in the leaves turning red. The degree of change in color depends on the amount of glucose stored in the plant. If photosynthesis has been occurring effectively until the start of fall and there is plenty of glucose stored in the leaves, they will turn a deep red. On the other hand, if there is only a little glucose in the leaves, the red will be a fainter color.

The Growth Pattern of Succulents

Think of leaves changing color and the next thing that springs to mind is probably leaves falling. For example, ginkgo and maple trees drop their leaves after turning beautiful colors. But despite changing color, succulents do not shed their leaves. Why is this so?

Leaves changing color and leaves falling tend to be thought of as a series of events, but in actual fact these are totally unrelated processes.

Deciduous trees drop their leaves in the fall to protect themselves from the cold and dehydration in the winter months that follow. However, succulents have come to live in unforgiving environments. In order to survive, their fleshy leaves have come to efficiently store water, sugars created through photosynthesis, and essential elements absorbed through their roots.

Of course, being plants, succulents do flower, but there are extremely few insects, birds or other creatures to aid pollination in their natural habitat. For this reason, they do not rely on their flowers to perpetuate the existence of their species, but rather have growing points throughout their structures where they can regenerate, sprouting new shoots from their leaves or sometimes from broken stems.

Succulents don't give out any opinions on the environment in which they're currently situated, they simply accept their surroundings and continue to evolve, and will keep doing so into the future.

A Little More About the Importance of Sunlight

Succulents need light in order to develop and grow, but how much light is necessary?

When plants perform the photosynthesis needed for their growth and development, the chlorophyll in their structures absorbs light of particular wavelengths. Mainly, it is blue (400–500nm) and red (600–700nm) wavelengths being absorbed, with the amount measured in a unit called photosynthetic photon flux density or PPFD (μ mol m-2 s-).

Light from direct midsummer sun measures 2000, when cloudy it is 50, and on a desk in an elementary school classroom it is 10 PPFD. As an elementary school classroom is meant for study, you would think of it as being bright even though it's indoors, wouldn't you?

Succulents need between 300–500 PPFD to grow and develop. We recommend placing them in the shade during midsummer because at the time of year the sun is too strong, but if they're not placed in direct sunlight during the rest of the year, they won't receive enough light.

Think of the light inside a building. On a fine midsummer's day there may admittedly be enough light by the living room window. However, on a cloudy day, the light outdoors measures 50 PPFD; indoors the PPFD will be even lower.

In the previous section we mentioned that one of the characteristics of succulents is that they don't fight their environment but rather adapt to wherever they're placed. If you place them somewhere where light is insufficient, they'll react by trying their best to reach the light, growing long and spindly in the process.

In the end, if there isn't enough light, photosynthesis cannot occur and the plant will not be able to produce energy and, like anything else, it will become exhausted.

As ultraviolet light is the mechanism which triggers changing of leaf color and plentiful sunlight from outdoors is necessary for accumulating sugars, unless they're in a specialized environment, succulents cannot do these things if kept indoors.

Cultivating and Planting Tips for Succulents by Genus

"I know there are many types of succulent but I can never remember their characteristics." We hear this a lot. Like all plants, succulents share the basic characteristics with others in their given genus. So as long as you know its genus, you will have a broad idea of a plant's preferences, shape and other characteristics. Here we have collated the succulents that are often used in Tokiiro arrangements. This should give you some hints for your own arrangement and cultivation of succulents.

TYPE	ATTRIBUTE	MAIN EXAMPLES	TIPS
Crassulaceae	Genus Echeveria	White rose, Secunda, Pulidonis, Party dress, Perle von Nurnberg, Chihuahualinze, Peacockii princess pearl, Powder blue, Sumirebotan, Frosty, Domingo, Mini bell, Runyonii.	The archetypal "succulent." Grows in a rosette formation to resemble a rose, with flamboyant, outspreading leaves. There are many hybrids and the genus has many fans. (See p30–31)
	Genus Aeonium	Haworthii Tricolor, Undulatum, Domesticum, Purple Crest, Lemonade, Sunburst	Grows aerial roots which become genuine roots once they reach the ground. Develops in winter.
	Genus Graptopetalum	Bartramii, Paraguayense, Bronze	Has fleshy leaves, and many varieties start to trail after a while.
	Genus Sedum	Rubrotinctum, Acre aureum, Pachyphyllum, Spathulifolium ssp. pruinosum, Japonicum 'morimura', Dragon's blood, Makinoi ogon, Uniflorum, Green pet, Mexicanum, Spurium cv tricolor, Adolphi, Oaxacanum, Morganianum, Makinoi.	More than 400 types exist. They grow in clusters, develop quickly and are relatively easy to grow. They love water and light. There are types that stand erect and stonecrops that cover the ground. (see p20–21)
	Genus Crassulaceae	Momiji matsuri, Mesembrianthoides, Capitella, Lycopodioides, Salmentosa, Expansa, Punctulata, Little missy, Tetragona, Ovata	Leaves grow in cross formations and the plant develops like a staff. Some types stand erect while others trail down, with the form of their leaves adding accent to arrangements.
	Genus Pachyphytum	Oviferum, Compactum, Hookeri, Pachyphtooides, Momobijin, Shireiden.	Leaves grow in layers. Cultivate in a spot that receives plenty of sun and is well ventilated.
	Genus Kalanchoe	Eriophylla, Kalanchoe tomentosa, Thyrsiflora, Pink butterflies kalanchoe	Well suited to the Japanese climate, this type is easy to grow. There are various types, with some covered in hair and some that change color.
	Genus Sedeveria	Letizia, Snow, Silver frost	A hybrid created by breeding Sedum and Echeveria, this genus has the characteristics of both these genii. Cultivate in a well ventilated place that gets as much sun as possible.
Liliaceae	Genus Haworthia	Obtusa, Cooperi var truncata, Cooperi var pilifera variegata, Cymbiformis var obtusa, Leightonii, Cuspidata, Cymbiformis, Turgida var pallidifolia, Retusa var, Cooperi, Turgida	Growing in the shadows of cliffs and beneath large trees, this genus has evolved to absorb even the smallest amount of light. Its leaves appear translucent, especially when held up to the light. Keep out of direct sunlight in summer but allow to get some sun on days of soft sunlight. (see p32–33)
Asteraceae	Genus Senecio	Rowleyanus, Prymidatuabar	There are many trailing types in this fast-growing genus. Roots grow wherever the plant is in contact with the ground, so the more ground surface it covers, the better it will take root. Loves water, so make sure it has plenty.
	Genus Othonna	Othonna capensis	Grows in the same way as plants in the Senecio genus but its flowers are of a different form.

Q&A: How to Grow Succulents Successfully

Whenever we hold displays of succulents or run workshops teaching how to arrange them, we are overwhelmed by the number of people asking questions.
A supposedly hardy succulent withered when they started looking after it, or the color faded away…

This section is a compilation of our most frequently asked questions. Now, how are the succulents doing at your place?

How much water do they need?

If they're placed in a spot where they can receive a lot of sunlight, water about once every two weeks to the extent that plenty of water comes out of the hole in the base. People grow succulents in various kinds of environments, so there is no hard and fast rule—check the condition of the plant and schedule watering accordingly.

While succulents don't need frequent watering and are easy to care for, if they receive insufficient water they won't be able to perform photosynthesis or transport nutrients through their systems. Plentiful light and appropriate watering are important. For more on this, please refer to p25.

Watering schedule

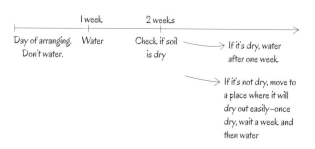

Where is a good place to put them?

Outdoors, in a spot with plenty of sunlight is ideal. The amount of light they receive indoors is nowhere near sufficient. Please refer to p86, 88 for more about light.

When should I repot them?

Succulents in the Crassulaceae family are mainly spring and fall growers, so spring and fall are the best times to repot them. In Japan in particular, around the times of the spring and fall equinoxes are probably best for repotting.

Is fertilizer necessary?

The fertilizer used at the time of planting should more than suffice for about two years. If you're topping up fertilizer after a while, use slow release fertilizer, available at home and garden centers.

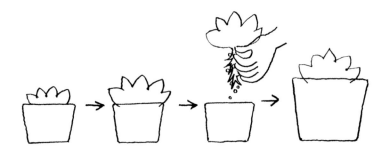

Is it OK if they get some rain?

Succlents hail from parts of the world that offer no protection from rain. Yet while these places receive little rain, it's not as if it never falls at all. So the answer is yes, rainfall is fine, but only for a day or two.

Beware of any particularly rainy times of year! Continuous rain weakens succulents. It causes the pores on their leaves to remain closed for a prolonged period, rendering them unable to take in the carbon dioxide necessary for photosynthesis. Three or more days of rain causes succulents to become stressed, and active oxygen is released in their leaves—basically, they attack themselves. In human terms, it's like getting a stomach ulcer from stress. Be particularly vigilant against rain during the night when pores are open.

When watering, there's no need to worry about water getting on the leaves—in fact, it washes away dust and dirt so to a certain extent, water is helpful.

What about when they get big?

Repotting will promote root growth, and allows for nutrients to be replaced, so it's a good idea.

Consider the condition plants are in when they "get big." We often have people telling us that the plant they took home was little and chubby and cute, but it quickly grew big and was no longer attractive. In cases like these, "big" usually means the plant has become spindly due to insufficient sunlight, making it grow vertically.

Most succulents use CAM carbon fixation pathways to perform photosynthesis (see p85), and it is said that their development is slower than other plants' due to photosynthetic response occurring in two stages during the day and at night. Sudden obvious changes in a succulent's leaves indicates that the plant is stressed and taking unavoidable measures in order to continue to survive. If, within a month of bringing it home, a succulent has grown significantly, look first at whether it is receiving insufficient light or whether it is being overwatered.

Our Own Journey with Succulents

We'd like to tell you about how we, TOKIIRO, became acquainted with succulents. That encounter led us to where we are, and continues to be our unflagging motivation on the path we tread today.

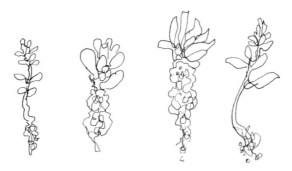

A married couple with no connections to plants or greenery, we encountered horticulturist Shingo Yagyu's succulent wreath when visiting Yatsugatake Club on the recommendation of a relative. Wife said, "I want it" but Husband said, "It will die, so we're not buying a living plant."

Wife really wanted it, so we bought a book by Yagyu that showed how to make a succulent wreath, and headed home.

The next day, Husband had the day off from work and dropped by neighborhood florists and home centers, buying succulents (which were not plentifully available at the time) and getting materials together, then referring to the book in order to make a wreath which he gave to Wife as a present. Wife was radiant with happiness. Her smiling face made Husband feel very happy.

After this, we made more and more of the arrangements and tableaux as per the instructions in Yagyu's book, until the backyard was full of succulent arrangements. There was nowhere left to display them and we weren't sure what to do with them. Soon they were spilling out of the backyard and into the front entranceway. People passing by on the street were starting to ask where they were sold, so we started taking orders and making them. Realizing we would be able to deal with plant markets, farmers and so on if we registered as a business, we decided on a business name.

The Birth of TOKIIRO

Taking time out to enjoy one of the many charms of succulents—the changing seasonal colors—this is the concept that led us to the name TOKIIRO (seasonal color). In the day-to-day we're so busy with work, responsibilities and so on that no sooner do we realize that the peak of the summer heat is upon us than we're shivering from the winter cold, letting the changing of the seasons just pass us by. If only we could take the time to truly appreciate each season.

Succulents have gently taught us about the seasons—and have made us more relaxed. We want to share that. This is what TOKIIRO is about.

Regardless of how much time passes, our concept has remained clear. We hope that TOKIIRO will evolve so that we can communicate the excitement and appeal of succulents to others. TOKIIRO started with a happy smile from someone close. Now we spend our days making things we hope will be the source of even more smiles all over the world.

To Our Readers

Succulents—including cacti and caudiciforms—attract attention not only in their countries of origin, but all over the world.

We think there's a reason that this single category of plants is so popular. Could it be that somewhere inside us all is a wish to spread these resilient plants across the world, to help counter the effects of environmental change? We all breathe and survive on the by-product of what plants produce for their own benefit—oxygen. If plants didn't perform photosynthesis, we wouldn't survive. If there were no plants we would cease to exist. Plants, on the other hand, could continue to survive perfectly well without people.

Thirty years have passed since the nuclear reactor disaster at Chernobyl, thirty years since people left the city. Toxic radioactive Caesium-137 has approached its half life, and with this have emerged images of the current state of Chernobyl captured by drones. These images are astounding in some ways as they reveal a "paradise" of plants and animals who have transcended human capabilities. In this city from which humans have disappeared, plants whose DNA is damaged continue to flourish, taking over structures built by humans, and thriving. This is the perfect example of plants accepting their environment, absorbing radioactive material and returning to the soil, leaving their offspring, and repeating the process over and over as if to protect the earth.

From ancient times, people have co-existed with plants, whose claim to the earth is older than ours. From them, we have gratefully received food, drink and even medicine over the years we have lived together. But the pursuit of mass production and mass consumerism, convenience and efficiency that has arisen from modernization has resulted in a gradual breakdown of the power balance between humans and plants.

What Tokiiro would like to tell people all over the world via the charm of succulents is to fix your eyes firmly on the future of people, plants and the planet. Consider things not only from a human perspective but also from the point of view of plants and the planet to create an environment we can all be part of. Why not make the simple act of placing succulents outside the first step towards this? It's with this thought that we will continue to devote ourselves to getting more and more people to understand the appeal of succulents, experience them hands-on and cultivate them.

Published by Tuttle Publishing, an imprint of Periplus Editions (HK) Ltd.

www.tuttlepublishing.com

TANIKUSHOKUBUTSU SEIKATSU NO SUSUME
Copyright © 2017 by TOKIIRO
English translation rights arranged with SHUFU-TO-SEIKATSUSHA,
CO. LTD.
through Japan UNI Agency, Inc., Tokyo

Translation copyright © 2018 by Periplus Editions(HK) Ltd.
Translated from Japanese by Leeyong Soo

ISBN 978-0-8048-5095-7

STAFF
Author: Yoshinobu Kondo (TOKIIRO)
Photography: Shuhei Tonami
Illustrations: Takayuki Fujikawa

Distributed by

North America, Latin America & Europe
Tuttle Publishing
364 Innovation Drive, North Clarendon, VT 05759-9436 U.S.A.
Tel: 1 (802) 773-8930; Fax: 1 (802) 773-6993
info@tuttlepublishing.com; www.tuttlepublishing.com

Japan
Tuttle Publishing
Yaekari Building, 3rd Floor, 5-4-12 Osaki, Shinagawa-ku, Tokyo 141 0032
Tel: (81) 3 5437-0171; Fax: (81) 3 5437-0755
tuttle-sales@gol.com

Asia Pacific
Berkeley Books Pte. Ltd.
61 Tai Seng Avenue #02-12, Singapore 534167
Tel: (65) 6280-1330; Fax: (65) 6280-6290
inquiries@periplus.com.sg; www.periplus.com

First edition
21 20 19 18   10 9 8 7 6 5 4 3 2 1

Printed in Hong Kong   1804EP

TUTTLE PUBLISHING® is a registered trademark of Tuttle Publishing,
a division of Periplus Editions (HK) Ltd.

About Tuttle: "Books to Span the East and West"

Our core mission at Tuttle Publishing is to create books which bring people together one page at a time. Tuttle was founded in 1832 in the small New England town of Rutland, Vermont (USA). Our fundamental values remain as strong today as they were then—to publish best-in-class books informing the English-speaking world about the countries and peoples of Asia. The world has become a smaller place today and Asia's economic, cultural and political influence has expanded, yet the need for meaningful dialogue and information about this diverse region has never been greater. Since 1948, Tuttle has been a leader in publishing books on the cultures, arts, cuisines, languages and literatures of Asia. Our authors and photographers have won numerous awards and Tuttle has published thousands of books on subjects ranging from martial arts to paper crafts. We welcome you to explore the wealth of information available on Asia at **www.tuttlepublishing.com**.